Memory Lane
Lincoln
and Lincolnshire

Memory Lane
Lincoln
and Lincolnshire

compiled by
Peter Washbourn

The Breedon Books
Publishing Company
Derby

First published in Great Britain by
The Breedon Books Publishing Company Limited
Breedon House, 44 Friar Gate, Derby, DE1 1DA.
1999

ISBN 1 85983 162 1

Printed and bound by Butler & Tanner Ltd., Selwood Printing Works,
Caxton Road, Frome, Somerset.

Colour separations by GreenShires Ltd, Leicester.

Jackets printed by Lawrence-Allen, Avon.

Contents

Introduction

MEMORY LANE. What does this mean for you? Is it times of half-day early closing in shops? Or the time when, if you caught a bus in Lincoln, you left from the High Street if you were travelling 'uphill' and St Mary's Street if you were going 'downhill'? Bus fares were 3d to go uphill but only 2d to come down! Bread was fourpence-halfpenny a loaf and you could get fish and chips for sixpence.

Whatever your memories, one of the best ways to recall many of them is through photographs. Many of us have our own photo albums, with cherished reminders of youth, holidays and special family events.

But it is through the newspaper photographs that many of the events of the years are remembered and at the *Lincolnshire Echo,* there are about a million of these images in the archives.

The *Lincolnshire Echo* was first published in 1893, but until the 1930s, photographs appeared very infrequently.

Major events, from royal visits, disasters of the day, through to childrens' parties have all been recorded by a team of photographers since the first staff photographer was appointed in the 1930s.

Many of their names will be remembered: Jim Haysom, Terence Fenby, Mike Hollist (now a photographer with the *Daily Mail*) and Cyril Middleton were on the team in the 1950s. The 1960s saw the team of Ken James, Stan Wing and Peter Washbourn together, a partnership which lasted almost 25 years, until Stan's death in 1984. Ken and Peter continued for another ten years.

Memory Lane Lincoln and Lincolnshire brings together a selection of pictures mainly from the period of 1930 through to 1980, although there are a few pictures from earlier years included. Putting this book together has not been easy. What to include and what to leave out? There will inevitably be questions as to why a certain picture has not been included. With only 450 pictures selected from a million, the answer is obvious – there just wasn't room. But if this volume proves to be popular, then more could follow.

Of course, all the pictures which appear in the *Lincolnshire Echo* are not taken just by the staff photographers. Frequently, pictures appear from the past which are loaned by individual collectors of such pictures. The *Echo* has been fortunate to have access at times to the extensive collection put together by Maurice Hodson, and Peter Grey also has a large collection of pictures. A few pictures from these collections appear in this book, having been used previously in the *Echo,* and acknowledgement is made to them. Thanks are also due to C. V. Middleton & Son for the use of a couple of pictures.

A book such as this is not the work of just one person. Thanks must go to Russell Kirk, Photographic Printer at the *Lincolnshire Echo,* who has brought the best out of many of the old negatives, and to Kevin Skaith, Graphics Manager, who is putting all the old images into a modern computer system to guard against the breakage of fragile glass negatives.

Finally, thanks to my wife Pat, for her patience while I have been surrounded by hundreds of pictures, and her help in reading through the finished captions.

Peter Washbourn
Lincoln
Summer 1999

How to order photographs
from Memory Lane Lincoln and Lincolnshire

Prints from which the *Lincolnshire Echo* hold the negatives can be ordered from the *Lincolnshire Echo* offices and all orders should preferably give the page number, first line of the caption and the RI number at the end of the caption.

We are unable to supply prints of pictures which do not have a number.

Prices (including 17.5% VAT) are:

7" x 5"	(approx) …£3.50 (in folder)	Postage.......75p
10" x 7"	(approx) …£5.00 (in folder)	Postage.......75p
16" x 12"	(approx) …£6.50	Postage..£1.65

No responsibility will be accepted for damage to prints sent through the post.
Cheques should be made payable to the Lincolnshire Publishing Company.
World copyright of all *Echo* photographs shall belong to the *Lincolnshire Echo*.

Photo Sales Department
Lincolnshire Echo Group Newspapers
Brayford Wharf East,
Lincoln. LN5 7AT
Tel: (01522) 525252 (Ext 218)

Memories of Lincoln

TAKING a trip through *Memory Lane* will mean different things to different people.

Lincoln has changed over the past century, but not so much perhaps as other towns and cities.

The Second World War did bring raids to the city but damage was not widespread, so much of the change has come in the second half of the century. A major re-development scheme in the 1950s was the construction of Pelham Bridge, to bring a road over one of the level crossing holdups. This saw the demolition of numerous rows of terraced houses in the area.

Another major scheme was the building of Tritton Road, from the city centre to the city boundary on the Newark Road. This time, the route covered more 'open' land, so little was needed to be demolished.

Another traffic-relieving scheme was the opening of Wigford Way, to bring a much-needed crossing of the River Witham and for this, some property in the city centre did disappear.

Many memories will be stirred by the pictures of traffic in the city centre part of High Street. Remember when the bus terminus for the uphill route was opposite The Cornhill? And if you wanted to take the bus to a route south of the city centre, then you queued in St Mary's Street? Also included in this chapter is a selection of pictures of some of the trade vehicles which were a familiar sight around our streets and roads.

A wintry scene at the High Bridge with workmen shovelling snow from the street into a horse-drawn cart in 1934. *(RI/559)*

One of the earliest *Echo* photographs, taken in 1931 from the window of Lincoln Guildhall, looking down a very busy High Street. *(RI/563)*

Looking up High Street in 1936, changes are taking place. The shop front under construction is for Hills and Steele Ltd., later to become British Home Stores, now known simply as BHS. On the left, Wyatt and Hayes, gents' outfitters, has gone today. A single-decker bus is pulling out from behind a double-decker with an open rear staircase. *(RI/62A)*

F. W. Woolworth and the Saracen's Head Hotel dominate the High Street, in 1952, with very little traffic. *(RI/421)*

The area of St Peter at Arches, just to the north of Lincoln Stonebow, decorated for the silver jubilee of King George V and Queen Mary, in 1935. On the right is the old Butter Market. *(RI/164)*

The same area of High Street two years later, garlanded for the coronation of King George VI. On the right is a poster advertising, 'Lincoln's first milk bar now open'.

Another royal event with the premises of Mawer and Collingham carrying flags to mark the coronation of Queen Elizabeth II, in 1953. *(RI/993)*

Cycles were very much the mode of transport for the working man when this picture was taken as the High Street level crossing gates were opening and some didn't even wait for them to be fully open. In the background was the garage, formerly the stables, for the Great Northern Hotel. *(RI/14)*

The roof covering Lincoln St Mark's Station was removed in 1957, leaving the platforms open to the elements. *(RI/850C)*

St Peter at Arches Church had stood in the centre of Lincoln for just over 200 years, when it was demolished in 1933 for street widening. Most of the structure was rebuilt as the parish church of St Giles. *(RI/927)*

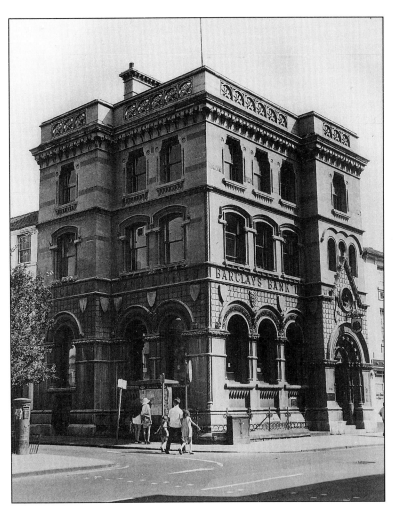

This rather splendid Victorian Gothic building, built in 1873 and in use as a bank, was demolished 100 years later to be replaced with a rather hideous modern structure of concrete, steel and glass. What a shame! *(RI/71/O/108)*

Prominent in the scene, at the corner of St Mary's Street and High Street, about 1946, is the Great Northern Hotel and the spire of St Mark's Church, both now demolished. Behind the tank, being carried on a transporter, is a horse and cart with the name of E. Nichol and Son, with the address of Abbey in the West, Foss Street, painted on the tail board. *(RI/260)*

Pickets outside the Lincolnshire Road Car's terminus off Lincoln High Street during a strike in 1957. Both the Royal Oak (left) and Lion Hotel public houses have now disappeared. *(RI/928)*

The bus station had only one road through it, so buses had to arrive and depart in the correct order. It was later replaced by a new bus station in St Mark Street.

There would appear to be nothing unusual about this Guy bus passing through the Stonebow, about 1960, but a look under the bonnet would have revealed a Ruston and Hornsby air-cooled diesel engine, made in the local works. *(RI/636)*

There may be traffic problems in Lincoln today, but it is highly unlikely that you would encounter a herd of cows being driven down the High Street like this scene in 1955. On the right is St Mary's Guildhall, erroneously known for many years as John O'Gaunt's Stables. *(RI/1862)*

One of the earliest sets of traffic lights in Lincoln, were at the junction of High Street and Dixon Street. When this picture was taken in the late 1930s, the bridge carrying the railway avoiding line over the street carried an advertisement for Allsopp's ales. Later, the advert changed to Bainbridge's and for many years, it was known as 'Bainbridge's Bridge'. Just before the bridge was removed, it carried the name of R-B, (Ruston Bucyrus), manufacturers of excavators.

It is not difficult to recognise this scene today, of Lincoln Cornhill, more than 60 years after the photograph was taken, in 1933. On the left is the Corn Exchange, built in 1879, and which was in use as the Exchange Cinema, showing at that time, a film starring Marlene Dietrich and Victor McLaglen. The Exchange Arcade, on the right, has advertisements for Hatton's Dining Rooms, offering 'quick service'. *(RI/79)*

Lincolnshire Echo's offices in St Benedict Square photographed in the 1930s at a time when the properties at the western end of the square, known as Crown Yard, were being demolished. The placards on the wall read: '3 children perish in fire'.

The old *Lincolnshire Echo* offices in St Benedict Square, which closed in March 1983, when printing was transferred to a new building on Brayford Wharf East.

Former warehouses on Brayford Wharf East which were demolished in 1982 to make way for the new *Echo* offices. Names of former occupiers of the premises included seed merchants, Mackinders and Beales's Warehousing and Haulage Ltd.

Saltergate, Lincoln, in the 1980s, before these buildings were swept away to be replaced by the Waterside Shopping Centre. Prominent in the picture is the Cannon Cinema, which opened as The Savoy, in the 1930s and later changed to the ABC Cinema, before taking the name Cannon. The Co-operative Bank has moved to new premises further along the street.

Lincoln Market, in 1933 looks more like a jumble sale, with trestle stalls and goods piled on them in a haphazard fashion. *(RI/73)*

This was the interior of the old market in Lincoln before the premises underwent modernisation. Above this part of the market was the old Exchange Cinema, which in 1957 gave way to a Roller Skating Rink (The Astoria) and, later, a Bingo Hall.

Saltergate, Lincoln, in 1900, was a narrow passageway formerly called Prison Lane. Jackson's, dyers and cleaners, still have a shop on this site. Although the buildings on the left have been demolished, there is still a public house called The Still on that site today.

Until traffic lights were introduced at the bottom of Lindum Hill, the 'bobby in the box' was a familiar sight directing traffic at a very busy junction. (RI/224)

The Bull's Head public house, at the corner of Silver Street and Clasketgate, in 1957. The tall building in Silver Street was the United Methodist Church, which opened in 1864. It closed for worship in 1940 and was demolished in 1973. *(RI/2210)*

Lincoln's first 'Panda' car at the old Sessions House Police Headquarters. Left is Detective Inspector 'Greg' Peck and next to him is Superintendent Tom Pickworth. *(E/407)*

A busy scene at Lincoln Cattle Market, in 1935. Today, the site is occupied by the North Lincolnshire College. *(RI/136)*

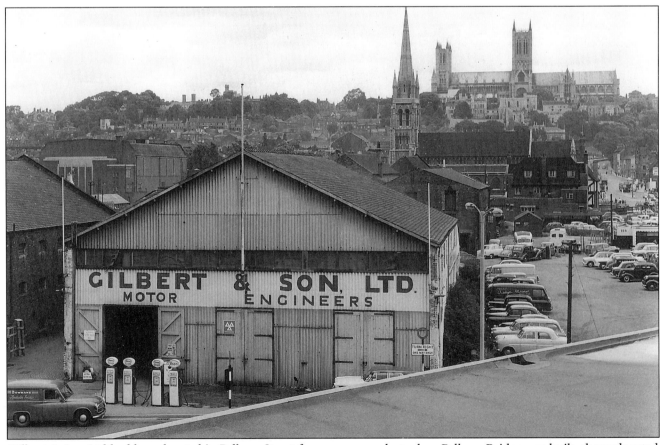

Gilbert & Son Ltd had been located in Pelham Street for many years, but when Pelham Bridge was built, they relocated to temporary premises in Norman Street, while new showrooms were being built and this picture was taken from these new premises. *(RI/4231)*

Since the 14th century, this old building had stood on Waterside and in later years contained small shops on the ground floor. In 1959, everything changed and it was restored into the Green Dragon public house. *(RI/2399)*

The interior of Lincoln Trustee Savings Bank, in 1957, presents a very different picture to the banking halls of today. No security screens and very little privacy for the customers. *(RI/1626)*

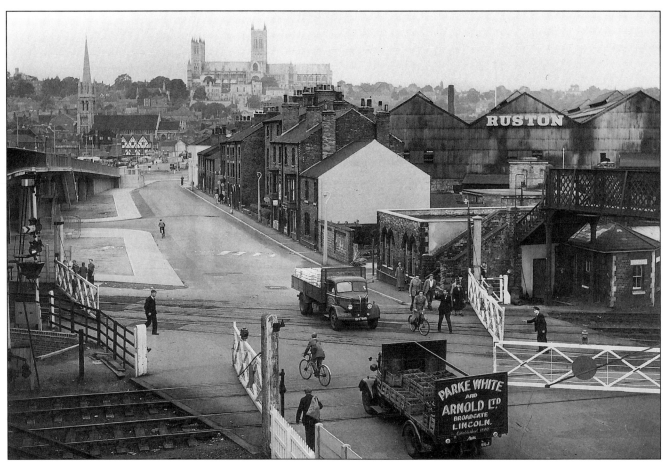

Pelham Street at the end of the 1950s, with the newly-built Pelham Bridge, on the left, the old level crossing gates, which were still in use, and the pedestrian footbridge over the tracks, on the right. *(RI/851A)*

Beevor Street level crossing with tracks leading into the old Midland Station, later to be called St Mark's. Today, all of this scene has disappeared with the development of Tritton Road and shopping parks. *(RI/850A)*

Work was in progress in 1936 building ornamental shelters in the grounds of the Usher Art Gallery, Lincoln, which opened in 1927. *(RI/64)*

Tests being carried out in 1961 to see if it was possible for double-decker buses to use the swing bridge at Brayford Head in a one-way traffic plan. *(RI/3237)*

Mazurska delicatessen shop, at Brayford Head, in 1955, was the forerunner of the now familiar 'deli' counters to be found in all major supermarkets. The shop later moved to premises in Guildhall Street. *(RI/2771)*

A large transporter having difficulty negotiating the old swing bridge at Brayford Head, in 1957. Only the Royal William IV public house now remains of this scene, the bridge having been replaced by Wigford Way. *(RI/2601)*

One of the hazards which motorists sometimes faced was the appearance of a swan in the High Street, having wandered there from nearby Brayford Pool. *(RI/3241)*

These houses in St Mark Street, Lincoln, have now vanished, but the building on the right, the former St Mark's Church Hall, still stands and is used by an animal welfare charity. *(RI/3322)*

Binks (Cycles) Ltd had their premises in St Benedict Square, Lincoln, from 1895 until moving to a High Street premises in the 1960s. On the left is the Thomas Cooper Memorial Baptist Chapel. The premises between the shop and the chapel were eventually used as a garage by the *Lincolnshire Echo*, from whose offices this photograph was taken.

Windy Blow, the clown, attracts quite a crowd in Sincil Street, Lincoln, with his decorated car in 1958. *(RI/3447)*

It would be difficult to recognise this scene today, taken in 1938 at the junction of Newport, Yarborough Crescent (left), Riseholme Road and Longdales Road. Work is in progress, possibly constructing a traffic roundabout. Note the coat thrown over the radiator of the vehicle on the right, to keep the engine warm. *(RI/196)*

Life for the residents of Burton Road was rather uncomfortable during roadworks and resurfacing in 1953. *(RI/1465)*

The demolition of houses on Steep Hill heralded a new look for the area, although it was to be a number of years after this picture was taken, in 1956, before any rebuilding took place. On the left is Jew's Court, which earlier had survived plans to demolish this important Norman building. *(RI/2221)*

'Join the AFS and CD' reads the illuminated sign on the roof of the building on Longdales Road, Lincoln, which served as a fire station until a new station was opened on South Park Avenue in the 1960s. *(RI/3818)*

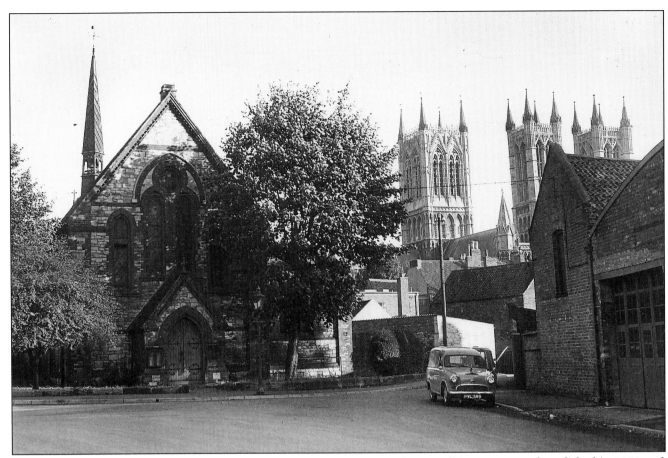

When this photograph was taken in the 1960s, St Paul in the Bail Church was still in use. It was demolished in 1971 and after archeological excavations on the site had been completed, the site was converted into a garden with some of the excavated remains on display. The old engineering premises on the right have made way for a restaurant. *(RI/999)*

Boultham Park Road with the bridge carrying the old 'loop line', which closed in 1982. The bridge, along with others on the line and the embankment have now been removed and the land used for building domestic premises. The ensuing street has been named Railway Park Close and Railway Park Mews.

Left and bottom left: 'Tidal flow' of traffic on Canwick Road, Lincoln, was introduced in the 1980s to help improve congestion at peak times. This picture shows the gantries for the signals being erected.

Right: It used to be quite a common sight to see advertisements painted on the walls of buildings, but this practice was generally replaced by poster hoardings. For many years, an advertisement for Blakey's Malted Oatmeal, a locally-produced product, could be seen on the end wall of a building in Canwick Road, Lincoln.

New life for old buildings. Pennell & Son's old seed warehouse and Le Tall's mill (the second tallest windmill in the county), in Princess Street, Lincoln have both been converted into domestic accommodation.

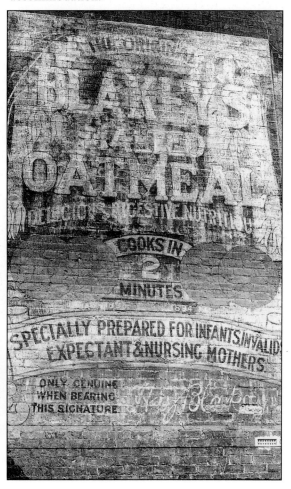

Boultham Baths being prepared for the opening of the 1936 season.

The floodlight pylons at Sincil Bank, the home of Lincoln City FC, provided a good vantage point for this picture of the high level avoiding line, with a background of rows of houses and factories. *(RI/2505)*

Hartsholme Hall, Lincoln, was built in the 1860s, but all that remains today is the stable block. It was at one time, the home of Lord Liverpool. During the Second World War, it was occupied by the military and was the Officers' Mess for 93 Company, RASC, 1st Airborne Division, Composite, which took part in the ill-fated 'drop' on Arnhem, known as Operation Market Garden.

The junction of South Park with High Street and St Catherine's was widened and a new roundabout constructed in 1958. This was in advance of South Park being extended into South Park Avenue, where new fire and ambulance stations were to be built. *(RI/3104)*

The opening of the first section of Tritton Road, in Lincoln, during 1967, brought about a much needed traffic relieving scheme into operation. Mayor of Lincoln, Alderman 'Jock' Campbell, cuts the ribbon at the opening ceremony. *(RI/3098)*

Waterside, about 1935. The building which was the Savoy Cinema is under construction. The building in the centre was the A1 Fish Shop, later to become The Witch and The Wardrobe public house.

A wonderful atmospheric picture of Brayford Pool in January 1939, when the water level was high enough to flood part of the road. *(RI/595)*

A moody picture of boat building at Kendall's Boatyard, Brayford Pool, in 1945. *(RI/246)*

There was plenty of activity on Brayford Pool at the Lincoln Boat Club regatta, held in 1962, an early forerunner of today's Brayford Water Carnival. *(RI/3215A/B)*

An 1899 Daimler, once owned by King Edward VII, with a 1935 Daimler, being used by West's of Lincoln for a promotion. On the front of the 'royal' car is a banner: '1899! See 1935 Models at Wests'. *(RI/508A)*

Trip Week trains about to depart Lincoln Central Station in 1960. *(RI/3317)*

Departing from Platform 7 is the last Lincoln-Retford train to run via Torksey, Cottam and Leverton, in 1959. *(RI/1328C)*

Lincoln Corporation's fleet of Dennis buses lined up, totally blocking the road, at the top of Yarborough Road. Advertising boards on the top of the vehicles carry well-known Lincoln company names: Lidgetts, C. J. Fox & Co and Jacksons; M. Culpin's grocery shop, on the right, has since been demolished.

A Lincoln-made Clayton steam railcar, made by Clayton Wagons Ltd, about to set off on a trial run to Woodhall Spa in the late 1920s.

The Railway Correspondents' Travel Society 'Ghost Train' pictured at Lincoln Midland Station (St Mark's) in 1954. The locomotive is a Midland Region 4-4-0 Compound. *(RI/1319)*

Vintage vehicle enthusiast Vincent LeTall and Lincoln Corporation Transport Manager, Herbert Jones, with a pair of vintage buses from Jersey Motor Transport Company, outside Lincoln bus garage.

A Vespa three-wheeler van, an adaptation of the well-known scooter, being used as a travelling bookshop by the British Christian Literature and Bible Societies in 1966. *(RI/3018)*

A familiar sight around the Lincoln area were the mobile shops operated by the local firm of A. W. Curtis & Sons Ltd. *(RI/3234)*

Smith's Crisps opened their Lincoln factory in 1936. This lorry was being used to bring in supplies of potatoes which were grown on the company's Nocton Estates. Smith's are now part of the Walkers Snack Foods Group.

A Hillman Husky van was used by Supreme Wallpapers for their deliveries in the Lincoln area.

Jointine Products were a well-known company of paper processors and this was their new vehicle in 1955. They were taken over by Wiggins Teape, who eventually became Arjo Wiggins. Sadly, the local factory has now been closed down. *(RI/2149)*

Edwin F. Smith's choice for a new van in 1960, was an Austin A35. *(RI/2396)*

City Electrical Company's Trojan van seems to have been in some kind of mishap when this photograph was taken in Ripon Street.

One of Foster's Transport fleet of lorries in 1956. *(RI/2235)*

E. R. Wright & Sons Albion lorries were used to carry many varied loads. Their depot was on Newark Road, Lincoln. *(RI/3727)*

'You move, I'll take you,' was the well-known advertising slogan used by George Barnes & Son on all of their removal vehicles. This picture was taken in 1947. *(RI/889)*

Memorable Moments

THERE are moments in everyone's life which stand out as memorable, for one reason or another. In this section, some of the events for which the century will be remembered come under the spotlight.

Royal visits have been made by every sovereign this century, although King Edward VIII was Prince of Wales when he came to Lincoln.

The Royal Show was held twice in the city before it was located on a permanent site at Stoneleigh.

Four coronations left the streets a mass of red, white and blue, for the festivities and some of the other events in the century are remembered in pictures.

One of the earliest memorable moments of the 20th century was the visit of King Edward VII and foreign royal dignitaries to the 1907 Royal Show, on the West Common, Lincoln. The streets were awash with flags and bunting and in this crowded High Street scene, five methods of getting around can be seen: pedestrians, a cycle, horses and carts, a car with a very early Lincoln registration (FE27) and an open-top tram, which only two years previously had replaced the horse-drawn trams which had been in use for 25 years. Lincoln's tram tracks were the shortest in the country, just one and threequarters of a mile in length.

The *Lincolnshire Echo's* van looks like a toy when compared to this pair of elephants in this picture taken on the South Common in 1934. *(RI/509)*

Coco the Clown makes friends with a young member of the audience during a circus visit to Lincoln. On his costume he wears many badges presented to him for his road safety work.

Lincoln greengrocer Len Talks got a bit of a shock when a passing horse poked its head through the doorway into his Steep Hill shop, but all that it wanted was a carrot. *(RI/1305)*

Shark and chips? Customers wonder which is the best cut from this shark which was on display at F. Bark's stall in Lincoln Market, in September 1958. *(RI/934)*

It would be difficult today to recognise this setting as St Mark Street, Lincoln, but in 1931 it was the scene of a procession for Lincoln Civic Sunday service. The mayor that year was William Elderkin, a prominent local baker.

The Auxiliary Fire Service had just been formed when this demonstration of their pumps was held on Brayford Wharf North, in 1939. The tall building in the background was Peel Bros, corn merchants. Today, the site is a multi-storey car park. *(RI/584)*

Students from Bishop Grosseteste College, Lincoln, march down Steep Hill to give publicity to National Education Week in November 1963. *(RI/1504)*

Ancient and modern side by side in 1955, with an old hand pump and the latest Dennis fire appliance on display in Lincoln Central Station car park. *(RI/2025)*

The Lincoln Salvation Army Citadel Band leaving Lincoln Prison in January 1958 after giving a concert to inmates. *(RI/1317)*

An old hand-operated fire pump was an unusual sight even in 1935 when this picture was taken in Broadgate, Lincoln. *(RI/561)*

Hunger marchers of 1934. Lincoln marchers are welcomed back to the city on their return from London while *(below)* a group of marchers from Northumberland near Lincoln are on their way to London.

Lincoln Salvation Army band play and collect money to help the Gresford Colliery Disaster Appeal in 1934. The mining accident, at the colliery near Wrexham, claimed 251 lives. The building in the background is the old Butter Market. *(RI/565)*

A coach and four attract quite a crowd, including three police officers, as it passes through the Stonebow, to publicise a Better Roads Campaign, in Lincoln, in 1956. *(RI/2202)*

No reindeer available, so Santa took to horseback to collect for the *Echo* Christmas Fund in 1934. *(RI/575)*

No wonder the children cried when they saw Santa, at Bainbridges store in Lincoln, at Christmas 1958. The sight of this Santa would have scared even the adults. *(RI/1272)*

A real live Nativity for this Christmas mime performed on the steps of Portland Place (now Central) Methodist Church, Lincoln, in 1957. *(RI/1273)*

The bells of St Mary-le-Wigford Church, Lincoln, about to be re-hung in 1932. *(RI/581)*

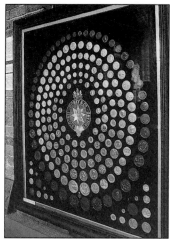

Lincoln's pride was its engineering companies, whose products won medals at exhibitions all over the world. Ruston Proctor & Co Ltd later became Ruston & Hornsby and are now Alstom. Robey's were well-known for their steam traction engines and Clayton & Shuttleworth boast wins at London, Vienna, Budapest, Prague, Krakau (Crakow), Lemberg and Crajove. These medal boards (replicas) are now on display at the Museum of Lincolnshire Life.

Lincoln City Transport Department decorated one of their buses to commemorate the marriage of Prince Charles and Lady Diana Spencer, in July 1981.

A Lincoln Corporation bus was decorated specially for the VE celebrations in 1945. In red, white and blue, the design, by the City Transport Manager, Mr George Rock, featured the flags of the allied nations. *(RI/555)*

A Lincoln City Transport bus was decorated in the 1970s to advertise Lincoln Theatre Royal. On one occasion, it was used to take a party of visitors from the city's twin-town of Neustadt an der Weinstrasse, to an open day at RAF Waddington, but the load proved too great for the vehicle, which was underpowered and it ground to a halt on Cross O'Cliff Hill. It was only possible to get started again when local hosts on the bus got off and rejoined the vehicle at the top of the hill.

The end of an era in 1905, when Lincoln's horse-drawn trams disappeared, to give way to new electric trams. This picture was taken at the St Benedict Square terminus of the journey and the young man on the left appears to have bundles of newspapers under his arm, possibly copies of the *Lincolnshire Echo*, whose offices and printing works were nearby.

Billy Smart's Circus arrived in town in 1955 and paraded from the Central Station to the South Common. Just look at those acrobats, performing their balancing skills on a moving trailer. The building on the corner of St Mary's Street and High Street was occupied for many years by Halford's cycle and motor cycle shop, but the 'Tudor' frontage is mock and the whole building has now been replaced with a modern structure, less pleasing to the eye. *(RI/1673 B)*

The procession of King Edward VII and foreign royal dignitaries passes down Lindum Road and Silver Street on its way from Lincoln Cathedral to the West Common for the Royal Show of 1907. Every possible vantage point has been used by the crowd, even ladders.

Lincoln had waited a long time for a road to be built over the railway lines in Pelham Street and Canwick Road, so there was a special welcome for Queen Elizabeth II when she unveiled the plaque to open Pelham Bridge, in 1958.

The Queen inspects a guard of honour in Lincoln Central Station forecourt in 1958.

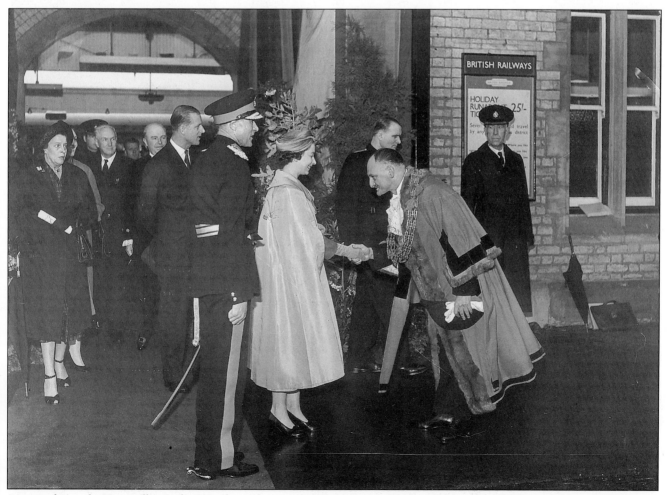

Mayor of Lincoln, Councillor Leslie Priestley welcomes the Queen to Lincoln for the opening of Pelham Bridge. *(RI/785 B 62)*

The obelisk on High Bridge, Lincoln, decorated for the Royal Show of 1907, which was held on the West Common.

High Street was a mass of red, white and blue for the celebrations to mark the silver jubilee of King George V and Queen Mary, and also the centenary of Local Government, in 1935. Note the fascia boards on Woolworth, proclaiming it to be '3d and 6d' stores and 'nothing in these stores over 6d'. Horses and carts were still being used for deliveries. *(RI/135)*

A procession of decorated vehicles down Lincoln High Street in 1935 to mark Civic Week, which celebrated the centenary of the Local Government. In 1835, the Municipal Corporation Act brought an elected council replacing the old Corporation.

The old Lincoln Corporation Offices, in Silver Street, decorated with flags and bunting.

Flags, banners and bunting decorate the White Hart Hotel, Lincoln, for the Royal Show in 1947. *(RI/666)*

Frank R. Eccleshare's offices were one of many buildings in Lincoln which were decorated for Queen Elizabeth II's coronation in 1953. (*RI/1109*)

The old meat market, in Lincoln Cornhill, decorated for the coronation in 1953. (*RI/800*)

The Stonebow, Lincoln, has for many years, been the place where revellers gathered to see in the New Year and there were both Army and Navy uniforms to be seen in this picture taken at the start of 1957. *(RI/2161 B)*

Auld Lang Syne rang out loud and clear as these revellers celebrate the arrival of the New Year, at Lincoln Stonebow. *(RI/1292A)*

The Dean of Lincoln, Rt Revd Colin Dunlop, watches as Lincoln's copy of *Magna Carta* is returned to the safe in Lincoln Cathedral in 1951, after it had been to the Public Records Office for preservation work. Also in the picture are the Chancellor, Canon T. R. Milford (at back) and the Clerk of the Works, Mr Robert Godfrey. During the Second World War, the charter was kept in America for safety. *(RI/817)*

Lincoln's copy of *Magna Carta.*

Before the clock mechanism in Lincoln. Cathedral's Central Tower was 'electrified', someone had to climb the steps to the clock chamber every day and wind up the weights by hand. For many years, this was done by Mr George Stowell, who had earlier checked his watch with the Greenwich Time Signal at 8am on the radio. The date, in Roman numerals on the mechanism, is 1880.

King George VI and Queen Elizabeth (now the Queen Mother), visited Lincoln in 1947 to attend the Royal Show, on the West Common. The king is seen presenting awards at the show. *(RI/413)*

King George and Queen Elizabeth arrive at Lincoln Station for the Royal Show in 1947. Mayor of Lincoln at that time was Councillor. H. H. C. Kerry. *(RI/413)*

The proclamation announcing the accession of King Edward VIII is read by the Town Clerk from a landau outside Lincoln Guildhall. Similar readings took place in other parts of the city. *(RI/499)*

An exhibition of royal memorabilia with ornate thrones and footstools went on display in the Usher Art Gallery, Lincoln, to mark the coronation of King George VI in 1937. The large canopied throne in the centre is from the Chapter House of Lincoln Cathedral. *(RI/503)*

Princess Alice, the Princess Royal, receives a bouquet at the opening of homes for retired clergy at Princess Royal Close, Lincoln, in 1957. Bishop of Lincoln at that time was the Rt Revd Kenneth Riches. *(RI/842/1208/A)*

Prince Philip, Duke of Edinburgh, looks around the kitchens after opening the NAAFI building in Park Street, Lincoln, in 1952. *(RI/ 842/RV)*

Remember These?

GOING up – or coming down? It has been said that more people will watch a building being demolished (especially by dynamite) than watched it being built.

But photographs tend to show construction rather than destruction, so there are pictures in this section recording the erection of buildings and structures, with just a few showing their removal.

One of the biggest projects in Lincoln was the building of Pelham Bridge in the 1950s. Since then of course and out of the time-period of this book, Lincolnshire and Humberside University has been started and is still growing.

Boultham Hall, Lincoln, during its demolition in 1959. It was built in 1874 and was the home of the Ellison family. During the First World War, it was used as a convalescent home for soldiers. Today, only the ornamental fountain in the foreground remains.

The obelisk had stood on High Bridge, Lincoln, since 1762, when it was erected to replace a wayside chapel on the bridge, dedicated to St Thomas à Becket. It was a conduit supplying drinking water, but in 1939 it was decided that it was too heavy for the bridge, which was by now carrying an increased load of road traffic, so it was dismantled. For many years, it was hoped that it might be re-erected elsewhere, but it was not until the late 1990s that parts of it were incorporated into a replica obelisk in the new shopping centre built on the old Midland (St Mark's) railway station site. *(RI/198A)*

Castle Hill House, in the centre of this 1930s photograph, was due to be demolished and the notice on the premises suggests that the site might be used for 'cinema, shops, cafés or flats'. In the early part of the 20th century, it was occupied by Dr Godfrey Lowe, a pioneer of motoring, and later became the home of the YWCA. To its left in the photograph, is the old Black Boy Inn, where the 19th-century public executioner, William Marwood, stayed during his official duties at Lincoln Gaol (then in the Castle). It is now Castle Hill Club.

Castle Hill House was under demolition when this picture was taken and the site, after being used as an emergency water reservoir during the Second World War, became a car park. *(RI/190)*

In 1941, when this photograph was taken, the site of Castle Hill House had become an Emergency Water Supply reservoir. *(RI/244)*

Today, the site of Castle Hill House and the reservoir is a car park. The telephone kiosk on the right has achieved the status of a Listed Building.

Despite the scaffolding, traffic still used the road through the Stonebow as workmen prepared the building for decorations to mark the silver jubilee of King George V and Queen Mary, in 1935. At the bottom left can be seen part of the name of Battles, whose chemist's shop occupied the site for many years. *(RI/135)*

Upheaval on Carholme Road in 1957, during the laying of pipes to carry telephone cables. *(RI/2244A)*

These pictures show the construction of a new bridge over the River Witham, in 1939, to replace the old Magpies Bridge, which itself had been built in 1858. The new bridge was renamed Thorn Bridge (the name of a 13th-century timber bridge at that site). The pictures also show the old Green Dragon Inn and the Lincoln British Legion club building, the former Magpies Inn.

With the introduction of double-decker buses, in 1927, it was not possible for these taller vehicles to operate on the Nettleham Road and Burton Road routes and use Pottergate Arch, as the single-decker buses had done, so the 'downhill' road was reconstructed to the left of the arch in 1937, and the road through the archway was closed to traffic. (RI/185)

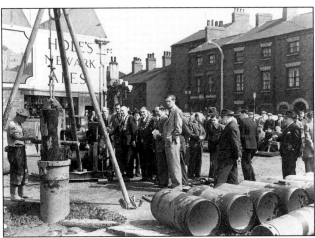

Mayor of Lincoln in 1955, Councillor William J. Bell, operated the machinery to drill the first pile for the construction of Pelham Bridge.

Pelham Bridge under construction shows some of the buildings in the area which have since been demolished. Bottom left is the Victoria Hotel and through the smoke beyond the curve of the bridge can be seen St Andrew's Church, which was demolished in 1970.

The Fire Brigade's turntable ladder gave access for these bird's eye views of Pelham Bridge under construction in 1956. There was little in the way of smoke control at this time, as evidenced by the many smoking chimneys.

Construction work in progress on the southern section of Pelham Bridge in 1957. On the right are houses in Canwick Road which were subsequently demolished.

Sincil Drain was one of the city's ancient waterways, with earlier banks which gave way to flooding several times. These new flood defences, giving a canalised waterway, were constructed in 1963-64. *(RI/4194)*

The old Mayfield Bridge, over the River Witham in the market area of Lincoln, was replaced with a bridge giving higher clearance for the passage of river traffic in 1957. Behind the crane is the old New Bridge Inn, which was closed in 1939 and used subsequently as the Red Shield Club and then the market manager's office. *(RI/1392)*

St Peter at Arches Church, in the centre of Lincoln, was demolished in 1933 and the main fabric reused in the construction of the new church on the St Giles Estate (which had been growing rapidly since 1922). On the right is Silver Street, and on the left, behind the church site, is the old Butter Market, itself demolished in 1937 with the façade being built into the new Central Market on Waterside South. *(RI/55)*

After excavation in the 1950s, the base of the tower adjacent to Newport Arch, Lincoln, built by the Romans 1,800 years ago, was excavated and left on public view. Unfortunately, today, the shrubs and trees planted on the banking have grown and partly obscure this interesting relic.

The steel framework of a new bus station for the Lincolnshire Road Car Co Ltd rises in St Mark Street, Lincoln, in 1958. (RI/1028)

Extensions were made to St Swithin's Power Station in 1947, and part of the massive construction can be seen in this photograph, which also shows the giant chimneys which were built of brick, rising from the top of the building. (RI/3382)

The new Road Car bus station in use after its opening in 1959, replacing the old terminus in the High Street. (RI/2874J)

Mothers with children in prams stop for a gossip as the prefabricated bungalows, better known as 'prefabs' were constructed on the St Giles Estate, Lincoln, in 1945. Originally intended only as a temporary measure, they later had brick 'skins' built around them to make permanent dwellings. *(RI/249)*

A modern stained glass window was installed into St John's Church, Ermine Estate, Lincoln, when it was built in 1962-63. The church was of unusual design by local architect Sam Scorer. *(RI/1467)*

Pupils from Our Lady of Lincoln Roman Catholic School line up for a photograph as the spire of the new Our Lady of Lincoln Church is lowered into place in February 1964. *(RI/2034)*

Taking shape in 1965 are the multi-storey flats at Stamp End, the tallest of three high-rise domestic buildings to be built in Lincoln, and named Shuttleworth House, remembering industrialist Joseph Shuttleworth, who built his engineering works on the opposite side of the river. *(RI/1633)*

Troubled Times Remembered

SOME of the most dramatic moments of the century were recorded in pictures by *Echo* photographers and a selection of these appear in this section.

Recalled are the floods of 1947, the storm floods on the east coast in 1953 and numerous fires.

The weather, in the form of heavy snowfalls also provides some dramatic pictures and reminds us of the fighting spirit of people to overcome these problems and disasters.

Winter takes its grip and a lorry is stuck on Canwick Hill in 1937. *(RI/544)*

There was help from a local schoolboy when the groundsman at Sincil Bank had to clear snow from the lines on the pitch in February 1953. No mechanical help in those days, just a shovel and wheelbarrow. *(RI/1717)*

Despite the fact that an ice-breaker had been through Brayford Pool, Walter Hall could not resist the temptation to use the frozen pool as a skating rink in January 1959. *(RI/1943)*

Only the swans were brave enough to venture on to the ice of a frozen Brayford Pool in the winter of 1936. In the background, on the left, can be seen the name Denby, a company which is still operating today, carrying freight to and from Europe. *(RI/97)*

No skates, but these youngsters still had fun on the ice in January 1954. Judging by the shadows, the photographer preferred to remain on dry land. In the background are the buildings on Brayford Wharf North and Lucy Tower Street. *(RI/1409)*

Traffic chaos on Lindum Road, Lincoln, followed a heavy snowstorm in February 1955. At that time, buses had a two-person crew of driver and conductor/conductress. *(RI/3800)*

Everything came to a halt when snow caused chaos on Lindum Road in February 1934. *(RI/560)*

Right: The severe winter of 1947 took its toll on Lincolnshire's roads and several feet of snow were recorded in many parts. Here, the main Lincoln-Sleaford road, the A1, has quite a covering.

Buses had to be dug out of the snow during the winter of 1955. This scene was at Hemswell. *(RI/890)*

Clearing the road by hand near Binbrook during the winter of 1947.

There was a lucky escape for schoolchildren, who had just been dropped off at a nearby school, when this bus driver tried to take a double-decker bus through Newport Arch in 1961. Fortunately, only the vehicle was damaged. *(RI/899)*

For almost 2,000 years, Newport Arch, Lincoln, had stood as a proud tribute to its Roman builders, but in 1964, it was almost totally demolished when the driver of a lorry, carrying a cargo of fish fingers, made a wrong decision and tried to take his lorry through the archway. The stonework had to be dismantled and subsequently rebuilt. *(RI/2032)*

A lucky escape with only damage to property when this lorry shed its load on the corner of Newland and Carholme Road, Lincoln, in 1965. The shops and houses in the background have now been demolished to make way for road improvements. *(RI/4160)*

Quite a crowd gathered at the junction of High Street and Mint Street when this lorry broke an axle in 1953. Its load consisted of full sacks with the names of London & North Eastern Railway, London Midland & Scottish Railway and British Railways. This was five years after the old railway companies were nationalised. *(RI/2388)*

There was a lot of disruption to traffic in Lincoln for several weeks in 1961, when huge girders passed through the city on their was to a new rolling mill under construction at Scunthorpe. Traffic lights and bollards had to be removed at many junctions to ease the way for the loads. *(RI/4035B)*

There was a full turnout by the Fire Brigade when fire broke out in the upper floor of the High Street premises of James Coombes & Co, footwear repairers, in October 1961. Many of the shops have changed use since then, but A. W. Curtis & Sons Ltd shop still remains today. *(RI/3302)*

Smoke and flames billow from Lincoln Co-operative Society's department store in Silver Street, Lincoln, in February 1969. This was the second fire in less than four years to destroy the premises. *(69/1715/8)*

The Fire Brigade have lots of unusual calls on their services and one was to a fire in a Lincoln Corporation rubbish collection vehicle in March 1964. *(RI/2036)*

Smoke pours from the Hovis Mill, on Brayford Wharf North, in August 1947, and the Fire Brigade use their turntable ladder to get water on top of the fire.

Schoolboys look on as firemen tackle a fire, possibly started by a passing steam locomotive, on the railway embankment where the Lincoln-Grantham line passed through the South Common, Lincoln. *(RI/1176)*

A fire at North Hykeham in 1955 severely damaged thatched cottages in Water Lane. *(RI/2386)*

It was not uncommon for barges travelling along the River Witham, through the centre of Lincoln, to get stuck under one of the bridges, either due to the vessels being empty or the river level being high (sometimes both together). The problem was usually solved by closing the floodgates at Brayford Head and letting more water out at Stamp End Lock. In this picture, taken in 1958, the former New Bridge Inn can be seen behind the bridge and a new footbridge with better clearance is under construction. *(RI/2758)*

Floodwaters from the River Trent encroach on to premises at Gainsborough during floods in 1932. *(RI/295)*

The Brayford Pool overflowed during a wet period in July 1958. Barges were still using the pool at this time as can be seen on the right of the photograph. *(RI/797)*

It is difficult to believe that beneath these floodwaters are the railway lines of Holmes Yard, Lincoln, during the severe flooding in 1947. *(RI/659)*

Beevor Street, Lincoln, during the floods in early 1947. On the right is Dawsons Belting Works and further down the street is the Excavator Works of Ruston Bucyrus.

Shoes off, trousers rolled up and briefcase under his arm, this man found a way of getting through the flood waters in St Andrew's Street, Lincoln, in 1947. *(RI/476)*

Problems at Brayford Head Bridge when the floodgates jammed during a period of high water in January 1959. *(RI/2891)*

Young cyclists seem to be making the most of floods in March 1955, when the River Witham overflowed into Brayford Head, as this stretch of road was called. *(RI/3866)*

People collecting fresh water which was brought in daily to various points of Lincoln during the typhoid epidemic of 1905.

A youngster and her dolly are carried to safety in the floods which devastated a large part of the coast of Lincolnshire in 1953.

Bottom, left: A stepladder, garden seat, table and planks make a precarious but safe way to evacuate residents from their flooded home.

Bottom, right: The full power of the sea can be seen from the damage to property in this picture of the aftermath of the 1953 floods at Mablethorpe. *(RI/10481 1D)*

The Duke of Edinburgh walks down the street at Sutton on Sea to take a look at the results of the 1953 floods. *(RI/1041)*

Vehicles stuck in the flood waters at Mablethorpe.

Memories of Youth

WHAT were your memories of youth? Was it visiting the circus? Or days in the Boy Scouts or Girl Guides? Perhaps you remember a particular party. How about the days of the Saturday morning cinema clubs?

In the time when there was no television and electronic games to occupy spare time, the street was your playground and the lamppost made an admirable set of wickets for a game of cricket.

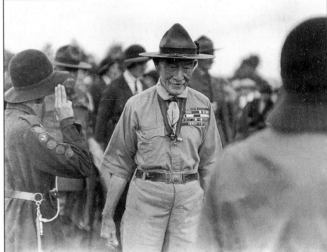

Founder of the Boy Scout movement, and Chief Scout, Lord Baden-Powell at a Scout and Guide camp held in the grounds of Hartsholme Hall, Lincoln, in 1936. *(RI/431)*

Scouts and Guides, led by the Scout Band, parade in Castle Hill to go to Lincoln Cathedral for their annual St George's Day Service in 1952. *(RI/2050)*

Lady Baden-Powell presenting awards to Guides at a rally in Spalding in 1954. *(RI/1385)*

Mayor of Lincoln, Alderman Fred Todd, and City Sheriff, Mr Fred Hunt, watch as two Scouts wash down the civic limousine during 'Bob a Job' Week, in 1959.

Steam trains were still running on our railways in 1954, when members of the Lincoln Model Engineering Society had tracks laid in Boultham Park, Lincoln, and gave rides behind their steam-powered models to local schoolchildren. *(RI/1869A)*

How many of us remember these days? The 'umpire' seems to have 'swimed' up the lamppost, which was being used as a wicket in this game of street cricket, with players no doubt keeping a wary eye open for the local 'bobby', who would frown on these activities in 1955. *(RI/859)*

It must have been a hot day when this photograph was taken at a crowded Boultham Baths, Lincoln, where the water temperature seldom exceeded 68°F (20°C). Far too cold for today's leisure swimmers!

There was plenty of snow for sledging in 1935, when these youngsters took full advantage of the weather to have some fun on the West Common, Lincoln. In the background can be seen Ellis' Windmill before its demise and subsequent restoration. *(RI/215)*

The pavement was the 'playing field' for these young boys for a game using cigarette cards. If these were not available, many would use the old cardboard tops from milk bottles.

A ring of sandbags around the lamppost at the junction of Skellingthorpe Road, Moorland Avenue and Rookery Lane, Lincoln. Known simply as The Junction, it was an irresistible playground for these youngsters and one appears to have fallen off, much to the amusement of the others.

When the April Pleasure Fair was held on the Cattle Market, Lincoln, in 1935, some of the roundabouts were hand-operated. *(RI/728)*

The April Pleasure Fair moved to its present day site of the South Common, Lincoln, in the 1940s and these youngsters *(above and right)* are seen enjoying one of the rides in 1955. *(RI /395E)*

A mile of pennies being laid in 1962, during the building of St John's Church on the Ermine Estate, Lincoln. *(RI/1433)*

The horses which have been grazed on the West Common, Lincoln, have always been popular with children, who were always keen to provide a few tit-bits, and Monty seems to be enjoying these in 1958. *(RI/1244)*

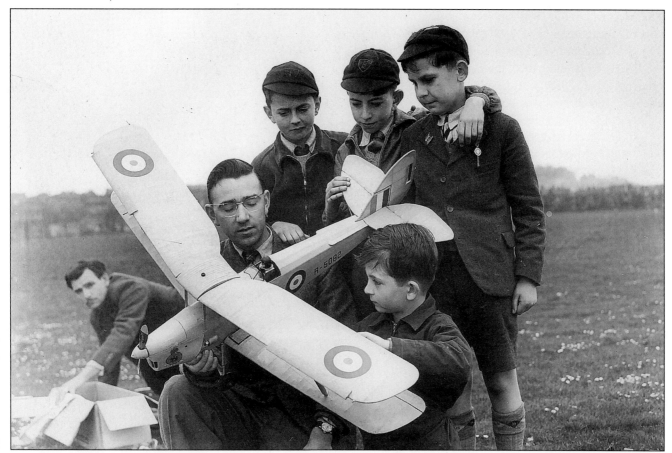

Wish we could have one! Young boys admire the model plane being flown by a member of the Lincolnshire Model Aero Club on the West Common, in 1953. Note the watch and chain in the boy's top pocket. *(RI/956B)*

Santa paid a visit to Mount Street Primary School, in 1955, to hand out goodies to the children. *(RI/1658)*

The Robin Dinner was an event enjoyed by thousands of youngsters over the years and was organised by the RAOB. In January 1900, the *Echo* reported that 2,000 children had attended the dinner and consumed 1,170lbs of beef, 1,550lbs of potatoes, 20 gallons of gravy, 250 breadloaves and 750lbs of pudding. This picture shows children queuing to get into the Drill Hall, in 1935. *(RI/549)*

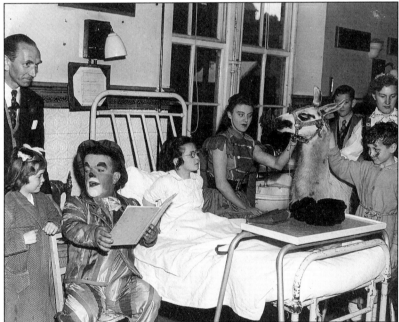

Chipperfield's Circus was in Lincoln in June 1957, and during that time, some of the artistes and animals went to the County Hospital to entertain children in Ruston Ward. *(RI/1131B)*

It was traditional for many local factories to hold a Christmas party for the children of their employees and pictured here are children at the party held by Clayton Dewarndre Ltd, in 1967. The company is no longer in existence. *(RI/2838A)*

Children of staff at the Theatre Royal, Lincoln, at their party in 1964, which no doubt included staying to watch the annual pantomime. *(RI/1522)*

Well-known Lincoln headmaster, Mr Jack Harrod, with members of West Parade Methodist Church Life Boys at their annual inspection and display in 1955. *(RI/1439)*

Pupils of Sincil Bank Girls' Secondary School, Lincoln, at their annual prizegiving. *(RI/2006)*

A cup of tea for mum and a chance for the children to show off their work at an open morning held at Hartsholme Infants' School, Lincoln, in 1953. *(RI/1505)*

Rosaire's Circus appeared at the Theatre Royal, Lincoln, over the Christmas period in 1953 and some of the performers went to the Savoy Cinema childrens' party to judge the fancy dress competition. *(RI/2839A)*

The Daleks put in an appearance at the ABC Minor's club, Lincoln, in August 1965 and got a mixed reaction from the audience. *(RI/3152A)*

A pair of Lincoln Corporation double-decker buses were needed to take members of Monks Road Baptist Church, Lincoln, Sunday School, on their outing in July 1957. *(RI/2222)*

Lincoln Infantile Paralysis Fellowship held their Christmas party at Hannah Memorial Church in December 1960. *(RI/2422)*

Children of members of the Lincoln Ambulance Service at their party in January 1964. *(RI/2042)*

Some are happy, some are not, at the party for children of members of the Lincoln and District Referees' Association, at the Black Swan, Lincoln, in 1967. *(RI/2836A)*

First day of term for the pupils starting at the Lincoln School in 1958. On the right is headmaster, Mr P. W. Martin. *(RI/2298)*

A real thrill for these youngsters who were allowed on the footplate of the engine pulling their train before their journey in Trip's Week, 1954. *(RI/1384A)*

Fancy dress was the order of the day for youngsters in Salthouse Lane at their street party to celebrate the coronation of Queen Elizabeth II in 1953. *(RI/823A)*

Military Memories

LINCOLN has been a garrison town ever since the Romans set up their military fortress here 1,900 years ago.

There have been two barracks in Lincoln in the last 100 years. The old militia barracks is now the Museum of Lincolnshire Life. The Sobraon Barracks, known locally as the New Barracks, has been largely demolished, but part remains and is used by the Territorial Army.

Lincoln gained a place in history during the First World War, when the first tanks were designed and built by Fosters.

In the Second World War, the city suffered some damage from enemy action and also was damaged by our own planes crashing, usually as they returned home from action.

Lincolnshire has earned the name of 'Bomber County'. During the Second World War, there were almost 50 airfields in the county. Now they can be counted on your fingers. Aircraft have always been a familiar sight in our skies for the last 80 years and a selection of aircraft pictures are included in this section.

Fourteen local clergymen who donned overalls and aprons to join workers at Ruston & Hornsby working to produce machines during the First World War. *(PW)*

Tanks of the 'Mother' type being built in Foster's factory at Lincoln during the First World War.

A church parade in 1931 was the occasion for these soldiers from the Lincolnshire Regiment marching down Lincoln High Street. *(RI/564)*

Members of the British Legion line up to honour the fallen at the Armistice Day service at Lincoln War Memorial, in November 1936. *(RI/713)*

Lincolnshire Regiment on parade with airmen and British Legion members at the Armistice Day service in Lincoln, in November 1938. *(RI/591)*

Armistice Sunday parade after the service in Lincoln Cathedral in 1938. *(RI/591)*

Workmen digging trenches for air-raid shelters near Monks Abbey, Lincoln, in September 1938, just one year before the war started. Onlookers wonder if they will ever be needed. *(RI/594)*

Members of the Royal Artillery giving a field gun demonstration on Lincoln's South Common in May 1939. *(RI/586)*

Members of the Home Guard lined up outside the Sun Inn, Saxilby. *(RI/606)*

The dreaded medical as county men line up to join the Royal Lincolnshire Regiment for their National Service in 1951. *(RI/8439-31)*

The front page of the *Lincolnshire Echo*, dated Sunday, September 3, 1939, announcing that Britain was at war with Germany.

Marjorie Blakey tries out the special baby gas mask on her daughter Christine in 1939. *(RI/489)*

Sandbags are piled up around the operating theatre at Lincoln County Hospital as a precaution against air-raids at the start of the Second World War. *(RI/569)*

A firewatcher looks out over Lincoln from his sandbagged shelter on the roof of the *Echo* office. *(RI/498)*

The first fatal casualty of an air-raid on Lincoln happened in March 1941, when bombs fell in the Baggeholme Road area of the city and destroyed St Swithin's School, as well as some houses. *(RI/497)*

A Hampden bomber crashed on Greestone Stairs, Lincoln, and the Christ's Hospital Girls' High School Boarding House in July 1941, one of six British planes which crashed inside the city boundaries, killing nine civilians, injuring 22 and with the loss of 18 crew members. *(RI/475)*

The heaviest air-raid on Lincoln was in January 1943, when 17 bombs were dropped. Houses in Thomas Street and Avondale Street were destroyed by the bomb which did not explode until after the inhabitants had been evacuated. This was the scene in Avondale Street. *(RI/253B)*

The scene in Thomas Street after the raid. *(RI/253)*

A huge crater and severe damage to houses in Westwick Gardens and Prial Close, Lincoln, following an air-raid in May 1941. *(RI/533A)*

A bomb disposal team with the unexploded bomb which was dropped on St Benedict Square in January 1943, causing disruption to the printing of the *Echo* until it was made safe. *(RI/254)*

These three pictures show the Nurses' Home at Lincoln County Hospital which received a direct hit by a bomb on August Bank Holiday weekend in 1942, from a lone German raider. *(RI/601)*

A pile of rubble was all that was left of St Michael's Church, Waddington, after being hit by a land mine in May 1941. Nearby cottages were also badly damaged and there was one fatality. *(RI/532)*

Shattered gravestones and damage to nearby buildings tell of the bombing of St Michael's Church, Waddington. *(RI/687)*

The bells of the church lie among the rubble after the raid. *(RI/687)*

A captured German Messerschmitt on display at Lincoln Station car park as part of War Weapons Week, in November 1940. *(RI/469)*

Air Raid Wardens on parade in front of the station during War Weapons Week in 1940. *(RI/482)*

An armoured train on display at the station during the week. *(RI/468)*

Fire tenders on display during War Weapons Week. Note how a private car has been converted into a fire appliance, towing a pump and carrying a ladder on its roof rack. *(RI/481)*

A novel way of raising money for the war effort was by sticking National Savings Stamps on a 4,000lb 'blockbuster' bomb on display at the Usher Art Gallery, Lincoln, in April 1943. *(RI/602)*

A recruitment campaign for the Lincolns in 1942 saw local engineers from Ruston & Hornsby Ltd taking part in the parade and passing, appropriately, the Broadgate Drill Hall, which was built by the founder of the company, Joseph Ruston, in 1890.

Women members of the Home Guard march past the saluting base at Lincoln's War Memorial in May 1944. *(RI/607)*

Crowds gather at Lincoln Stonebow in May 1945 to celebrate Victory in Europe. *(RI/578)*

It's all over. A surface air-raid shelter in Walmer Street, Lincoln, decorated with a symbolic painting after the end of hostilities in August 1945. *(RI/727)*

Thanksgiving Week in October 1945 saw people decorating prams to mark the end of Second World War. *(RI/556)*

Civil Defence was still very much on people's minds in 1957, when this exercise was taking place at Lincoln Power Station, with workers from Smith Clayton Forge taking part. *(RI/1374)*

Members of the Womens' Land Army march through Lincoln to a special Victory in Europe service at Lincoln Cathedral just one week after the ending of hostilities. *(RI/578)*

The opening of the British Legion Club in Lincoln, was marked by an inspection of veterans in August 1946. *(RI/723)*

Inspection time for members of the Womens' Land Army, on the South Common, Lincoln, in 1946. *(RI/263)*

The 2nd East Anglian Regiment, into which the Royal Lincolnshire Regiment was incorporated, march up Lincoln High Street in April 1961. *(RI/4044A)*

Soldiers of the Royal Lincolnshire Regiment line up before the city's War Memorial during a parade in May 1953. *(RI/849-8)*

Lincoln Central Station was the departure point for troops of the Royal Lincolnshire Regiment as the advance contingent leave for service in Minden, Germany, in 1958. *(RI/849-17)*

The first Ruston built aircraft in the First World War was flown by Captain Tennant and attracted a lot of attention. It was a Ruston-built plane which shot down the first German raider, a Zeppelin, to be brought down on British soil. The pilot was awarded the VC. *(PW)*

Forerunners of today's Red Arrows, the Cobham Flying Circus is seen in the air over the Burton Road-Yarborough Road area of Lincoln, in 1933. *(RI/5O5)*

One of the Royal Air Force's fleet of bombers pictured at RAF Waddington in 1934. *(RI/506)*

Refuelling time for a group of Hawker light bombers at RAF Digby in 1935. *(RI/419)*

Airmen learning how to maintain a radial engine at RAF Digby in 1935. *(RI/945)*

The City of Lincoln Lancaster and a Vulcan Bomber fly over Lincoln in 1968. Both types of aircraft saw service with 617 Squadron, The Dam Busters. *(RI/l460)*

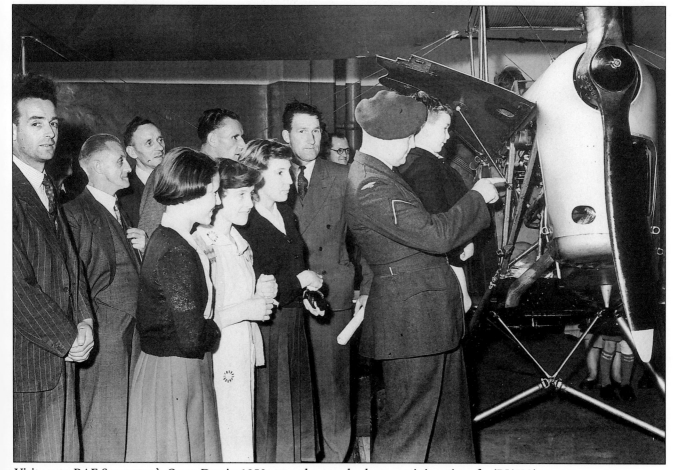

Visitors to RAF Scampton's Open Day in 1953 get a close up look at a training aircraft. *(RI/422)*

Crew members of Jamaica Squadron, at RAF Hemswell in the 1960s, check flight plans before leaving on a tour of Canada and Jamaica. *(RI/958)*

Canberra Bombers of Jamaica Squadron lined up at RAF Hemswell. *(RI/958)*

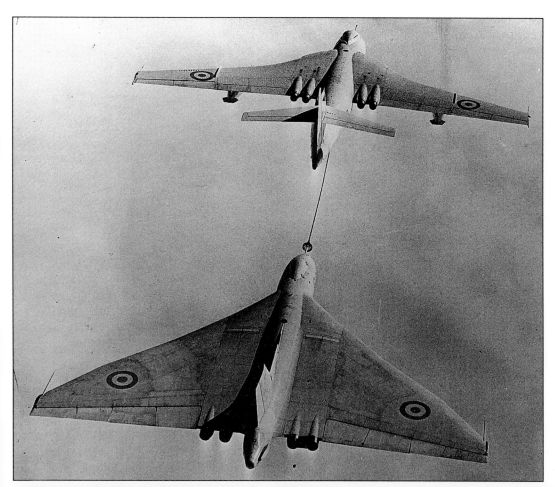

In-flight refuelling for this Vulcan Bomber from a Victor Tanker aircraft. Both types of aircraft were a familiar sight in the skies over Lincolnshire. *(RI/967)*

Veterans of the Second World War, the Spitfire and Hurricane gave a display at RAF Waddington's Open Day in 1961. *(RI/960)*

A pair of Shackleton reconnaissance aircraft seen at an air display in Lincolnshire.

It looks like families day for 50 Squadron at RAF Waddington, in 1966, with a Lightning and Dominie aircraft under inspection. *(RI/963)*

Forerunner of the Vulcan bomber, the Avro Delta 707A, photographed in 1953. *(RI/954)*

The Duke of Edinburgh was a proud parent at RAF Cranwell in 1971 when Prince Charles attended the college and passed out having won his wings. *(RI/842PC)*

'Farewell' is the message painted on the inside of the bomb bay doors of the last Vulcan flying over Lincoln.

Farewell to the city. The RAF's last Vulcan bomber flies over Lincoln Cathedral on its farewell flight.

An E3 sentry aircraft, better own as an 'AWAC', carries the City of Lincoln crest on its fuselage.

The Battle of Britain Memorial flight, of Lancaster, Spitfire and Hurricane, a familiar sight in the Lincolnshire skies.

Gate guardian at RAF Scampton for many years, this Lancaster bomber is now at the RAF Museum, Hendon. Another Lancaster, which followed this one, is now at the Lincolnshire Aviation Heritage Centre, at East Kirkby. *(RI/2192)*

A disastrous end for this Lincoln bomber which crashed at Hemswell in 1955. Fuel is being unloaded from the tanks. *(RI/1683B)*

Community Relations Officer at RAF Waddington, Flight-Lieutenant Joe 'Spike' Hughes, checks his watch as he leads out a group of pressmen for an event at the base. Nearest the camera is *Echo* photographer Peter Washbourn and on the right, with cine camera is Cyril Middleton, who was filming for Anglia Television. The date is sometime in the 1960s. *(CVM)*

Lining up on a wet runway are English Electric Lightning bombers at RAF Binbrook.

Nine Avro Vulcan bombers in their all-white colouring, later to be camouflaged, on the runway at RAF Scampton, for *Exercise Mayflight* in 1961. *(RI/3309B)*

A Vampire jet fighter on the runway at the old RAF Skellingthorpe airfield in 1955. The airfield is now a part of the Birchwood Estate, Lincoln. *(RI/959)*

Memories Are Made Of These

LOOKING through the *Echo* archives, one cannot help but notice the number of pictures of people, rather than events.

From the late 1940s, through to the 1960s, the *Lincolnshire Echo* produced a weekly picture edition, better known as the 'Pic-Echo' and this mirrored the local scene of parties, dances and weddings.

From time to time, celebrities have visited the area and in the 1950s and 1960s, there were regular concerts and shows by top artists from the world of pop music.

There are also some pictures taken of some of the local personalities who have coloured our lives during the past few decades.

Echo chief photographer Ken James's picture of The Beatles was used by the Tokyo Beatles Fan Club for their magazine cover in 1992.

The Beatles – George Harrison, John Lennon, Paul McCartney and Ringo Starr – took Lincoln by storm, when they appeared at the ABC to give concerts in November 1963. *(RI/782-B)*

Singer Anthony Newley signs autographs for workers at Smith's Crisps Lincoln factory during a visit in February 1960. *(RI/3595-B)*

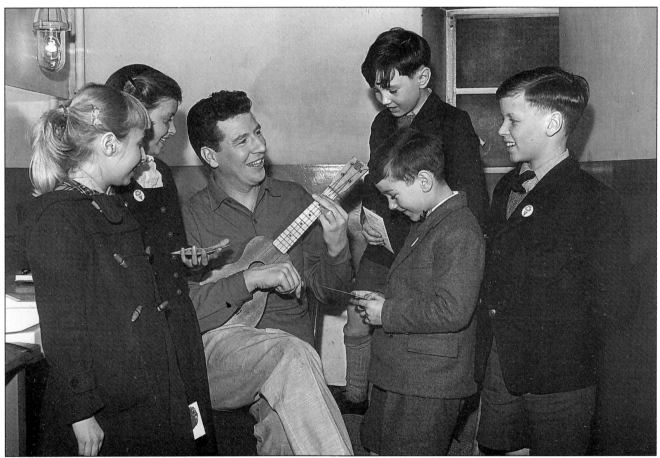

Max Bygraves appeared at the ABC Lincoln in 1959 and during that visit, he met young fans from the ABC Minors' Club backstage in the dressing room. *(RI/444)*

Heart-throb Adam Faith was the centre of attraction for a group of admirers when he appeared at the Castle Club at RAF Coningsby, in October 1963. *(RI/2345A)*

Singer Michael Holliday visited the *Echo* offices in 1958 when appearing at the ABC Lincoln. He is pictured signing autographs for staff and seeing how the paper was produced. *(RI/3505 A&B)*

Gerry and the Pacemakers made their mark with the song *You'll Never Walk Alone*, which has almost become the national anthem for Merseysiders, but the song was a hit long before their version, coming from the musical *Carousel*. The group visited Lincoln in November 1963. *(RI/2951A)*

Helen Shapiro signs autographs for Patricia Roberts and John Middleton during her appearance at the ABC Cinema, Lincoln, in 1962. *(RI/3918A)*

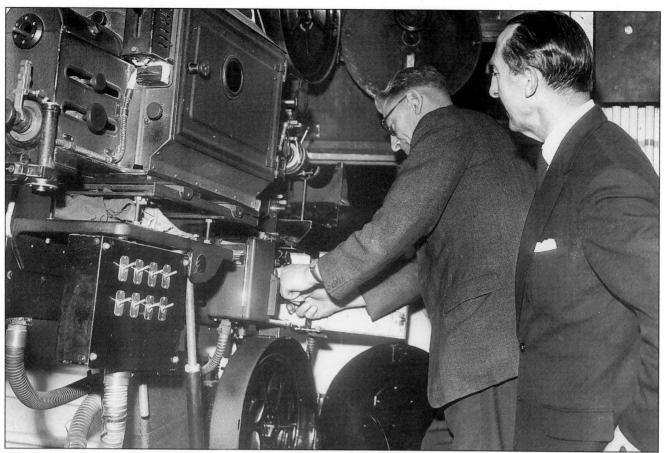

A behind-the-scenes look at the projector as it is loaded for the last time at the Regal Cinema, Lincoln, which closed in February 1966. Loading up the machine is projectionist Sid Whitelam, watched by manager, Mr Ritter. *(RI/709/A334)*

The queue of fans waiting to see *Rock Around The Clock* when the film was screened at the Regal Cinema, Lincoln, in September 1956, stretched from the cinema, down the High Street to St Benedict Square. *(RI/2125C)*

Some fans were prepared to spend all night waiting for the box office to open at the ABC when Billy Fury was due to appear in 1962. *(RI/4213-B)*

Local beauty competitions were a regular feature of life in the 1950s and 1960s and pictured here are the contestants in the Miss Lincoln competition, held at the Broadgate Drill Hall in 1963. *(RI/3059C)*

Some of the contestants in a beauty competition held at the Court School of Dancing, Lincoln, in 1958. *(RI/3438)*

A teenage party at St Hugh's Church Hall, North Hykeham, in 1963, saw young people dancing to the beat of local live music. *(RI/1526B)*

Hooped skirts were all the rage in 1959, when members of the Happy Circle Jive Club held their Christmas party at Newport Co-op Hall, Lincoln. *(RI/2817B)*

The Happy Circle Jive Club members at their party. *(RI/2817A)*

Let's do The Twist. Bailgate Youth Club members at their social evening in 1963. *(RI/1521)*

Lincoln Thespians Operatic Society rehearsing for their production of *No, No, Nanette* in 1937. *(RI/545)*

Panto time? Oh yes it is! *The Old Woman Who Lived In A Shoe* was the entertainment at Christmas time at the Theatre Royal, Lincoln, in 1954. *(RI/1957)*

Blossom Time was the production presented by the Lincoln Amateur Operatic and Dramatic Society at the Theatre Royal, Lincoln, in 1939. *(RI/579)*

The City School, Lincoln (now the City of Lincoln Community College) always enjoyed the reputation of having a good orchestra. This picture was taken in 1935 and some of the school's staff will be remembered by many. Top right is Canon 'Ozzie' Jones. In front of him are Bill Brocklehurst (viola), and to his right are Alf Beedham (trombone), Frank Clarke (cello). 'Jock' Hadden is on the double bass and Freddie Andrews on timpani. 'Ash' Holmes played the clarinet. *(RI/571)*

Ruston Engineers' Prize Silver Band played for a *Work's Wonders* radio broadcast from Ruston's Canteen in 1951. Musical director of the band was Cyril Racey (left) and seated fourth from left is Geoff Moralee MBE, who is the current musical director of Lincoln Beevor Band, having been in banding for more that 60 years. Indeed, Geoff was awarded the MBE for his services to banding. *(RI/930)*

Actor Bill Maynard, better known today as Claude Greengrass in *Heartbeat*, has his eye on the pocket, as usual, but this time on the billiards table during a visit to Sincil Bank, where he met members of Lincoln City FC, including their long-serving manager, Bill Anderson (second from right) in 1959. *(RI/1394)*

Lincoln 'campaigner' Clarence Hurst (left) with supporters setting off for London in 1972 with one of many petitions. *(RI/1342)*

Mayor of Lincoln, Councillor Dr Charles Lillicrap, with Henry Tyler and 'Snips', who was presented with many medals for collecting money for charity, this time for Hungarian Relief, in 1957. *(RI/3792A)*

'Snips' the dog which collected money for charity on a stall in Lincoln Market being stroked for a penny a time by youngsters. *(RI/1243D)*

Lincoln-born TV personality Steve Race signs autographs for local youngsters.

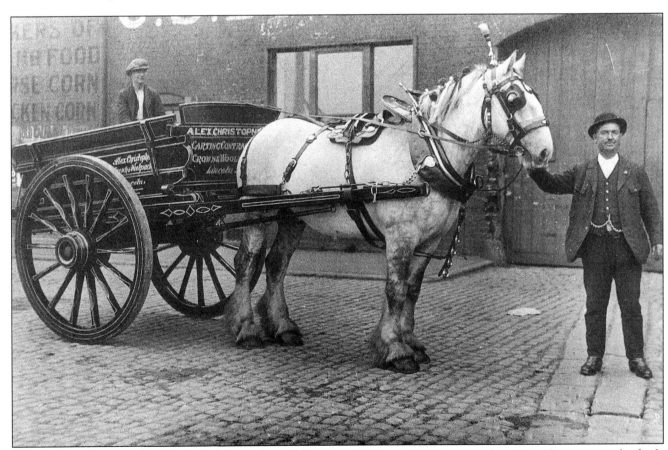

Alex Christopher was a familiar sight in Lincoln in the 1930s and 40s, with his horse and cart. He always sported a fresh flower every day in his buttonhole. He was a dealer in horse-flesh and lived in a former well-known Lincoln public house, the Crown and Woolpack.

The name of 'Skipper' Ross was a legend in Lincoln during the 1950s and early 1960s, when with his boat, the *Mary Gordon*, he gave pleasure trips to thousands around the Brayford Pool, Lincoln.

A notice in the city directing visitors to the *Mary Gordon*.

Lincoln Theatre manager in 1952, Raymond Bennett was a big man, but not tall. Wee Georgie Wood was a big man in entertainment, but not in stature. *(RI/1159)*

Prime Minister Clement Atlee on the balcony of the old Thornbridge Hotel, Lincoln, during the General Election campaign of October 1951, where he was speaking on behalf of the Lincoln Labour candidate, Geoffrey de Freitas. *(RI/654)*

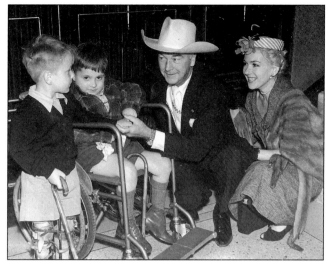

A hero of Saturday morning cinema clubs with children everywhere was actor William Boyd, better known as 'Hopalong Cassidy', who visited Lincoln in 1954. *(RI/1304)*

Staff at Lincoln Sorting Office dealing with the Christmas rush of letters in December 1957. *(RI/2238 A&B)*

'Hopalong' waves to the crowds who had turned out to see him. *(RI/1304)*

The well-known and much loved Canon 'Ozzie' Jones receiving donations at St Mark's Church, Lincoln, first gift day, in 1955. *(RI/1448)*

Families at Lincoln LNER (Central) Railway Station, in 1931, waiting for the train to take them on their Trip's Week holiday. *(RI/548)*

The friendly Railway Police 'bobby' with a group of holidaymakers setting out from Lincoln Central Station during Trip's Week in 1953. *(RI/830A)*

King of the castle… a young lad ready for the beach as he sits on a mountain of suitcases while waiting for the train in Trip's Week, 1954. *(RI//384B)*

Crowds queue at Lincoln Central Station in 1956, to wait for the trains taking them on their annual holiday. Note the W. H. Smith's bookstall, a still-familiar sight at most larger railway stations. *(RI/1873)*

A popular spot for a 'chin-wag' are the seats on High Bridge, Lincoln, where some of the local senior citizens gathered to put the world to rights in 1959. *(RI/2756)*

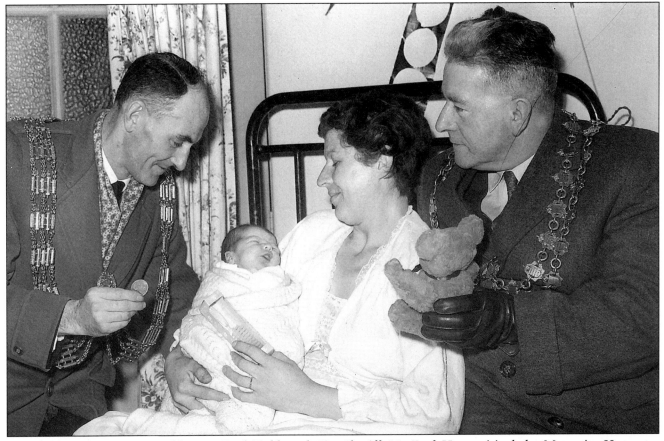

Mayor of Lincoln in 1959, Alderman Fred Todd, and City Sheriff, Mr Fred Hunt, visited the Maternity Home on Christmas Day and presented a traditional gift of a crown coin (five shillings or 25p today) to a baby who had been born only hours earlier. *(RI/2819A)*

Canon Victor Dalby joins Father Christmas and helpers at St Giles's Church, Lincoln, during the Christmas Fayre in 1955. *(RI/3169)*

Lincoln Imps Hockey Club members and guest at their annual dance in November 1953. *(RI/1609)*

Staff of the *Lincolnshire Echo* get together for their annual dance at the Co-operative Ballroom, Lincoln, in 1951. Staff members who can be identified are photographer Stan Wing (front row, second from left), Bernard O'Connor (middle row, right) and Les Jackson (back row, right) who was also the organist with a local dance band. *(RI/2131)*

Jackson's Laundry staff and their families went to Cleethorpes for their annual outing in 1954. *(RI/3497)*

St Botolph's Church Hall was the venue for the annual dance held by Lincoln Ballroom Dancing Club, in 1959. *(RI/2816)*

Hunting for bargains at St John Ambulance Brigade's Christmas Fayre, in 1955. *(RI/3175)*

Residents of Coleridge Green went to Cleethorpes for an outing in June 1953. *(RI/1353)*

Lincoln's Police Force pose for this group photograph in the 1880s. The background is the magnificent conservatory which stood on the terrace in Lincoln Arboretum. *(RI/799)*

Members of the Lincoln Musical Society under the baton of Cathedral organist Dr Gordon Slater, rehearsing St Matthew's Passion in 1953. *(RI/1618)*

Harold and Mary Wilson with members of Lincoln Labour Party during the Prime Minister's visit in 1969. At the back, in the centre, is Dick Taverne, who was Labour MP for Lincoln at that time before his split with the party. *(J/149/24)*

Prime Minister Harold Wilson, with Bill and Eileen Herbert, during a visit to the city in 1969. Bill and Eileen had been Mayor and Mayoress of Lincoln in 1961. *(J/149/2)*

In 1973, Dick Taverne (second from right) split from the Labour Party, stood for Parliament in a by-election as Democratic Labour and won. He is seen here with supporters including journalist Bernard Levin (second left) and the Rt Revd Mervyn Stockwood, Bishop of Southwark (centre). *(9021B)*

In 1972, members of the Feucht Frohliche Neustadters (FFN), a wine appreciation society from Lincoln's twin-town in Germany, planted a vineyard at the Bishop's Old Palace, to commemorate the 900th anniversary of Lincoln Cathedral. Centre of this group is the late Hermann Weiss, publicity officer for Neustadt, and cleaning his shoes is Manfred Arnecke. *(PW)*

A familiar sight in Lincoln for many years was the figure of 'Briggy'. Leslie Briggs was employed by the council until his retirement as a roadsweeper and in his later years he could be seen 'busking' for coppers. The only trouble was, he couldn't play a note, only make a sound, from his mouth organ. *(PW)*

Jim Russell was Lincoln mayor's officer for many years and one of his duties was to carry the King Richard II sword before the mayor in civic processions. The sword was presented to the city in 1386 by King Richard and is traditionally handed back to the sovereign when they visit the city, for it to be re-presented. *(PW)*

Memorable County

LINCOLNSHIRE is an enormous county. If you set out for London from its northernmost point, you are halfway there before you leave the county.

Echo photographers have had to cover events in this vast area and just a few of their pictures are shown here.

In an agricultural county such as ours, there are plenty of pictures to be taken showing the working of the land and there are reminders of days when power came from nature, rather than by combustion engine.

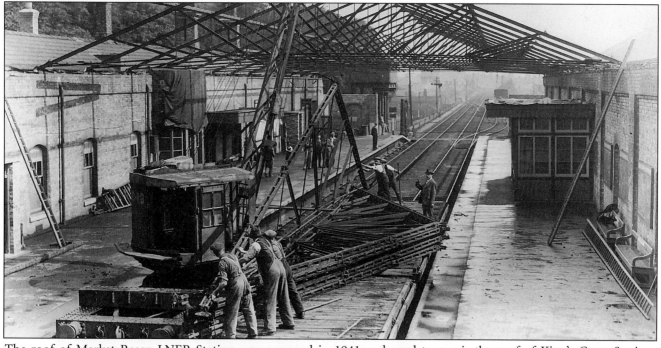

The roof of Market Rasen LNER Station was removed in 1941 and used to repair the roof of King's Cross Station, London, after it had been damaged in an air-raid. A Ruston-Bucyrus 10RB crane has been specially mounted on a railway bolster wagon to do the work. *(RI/398)*

Schoolchildren in Horncastle out for a walk in 1959. *(RI/2635 B)*

Bayon's Manor, Tealby, was built by Charles Tennyson d'Eyncourt in 1836-42, but in 1965 it was demolished when the property company which had bought it could not find a buyer. What a shame! *(RI/347)*

Gainsborough Old Hall had a rather run-down look about it when this photograph was taken in 1947. Today, it is the pride of Gainsborough and one of the finest buildings of its period in the country. *(RI/405A)*

A line up of bathing beauties at Butlin's Holiday Camp, Skegness, for the Holiday Princess Contest in 1959. *(RI/2761A)*

An old stage coach providing a platform for youngsters enjoying a holiday at Butlin's, Skegness, in 1959. *(RI/2760)*

Ropery Road, Gainsborough, under water during floods in 1947. *(RI/401)*

Louise the Lamb came to the kitchen window at Waves Farm, Saxilby Road, Lincoln, whenever she felt hungry. *(RI/1127)*

A large sale of farm machinery and parts was held at Fiskerton Airfield in November 1956. *(RI/1558)*

Tea Pot Cottage, near Dalderby, was a most unusual sight before its demolition. *(RI/350)*

It would be difficult today to realise that this is Bridge Street, Gainsborough. The prominent building was known as Pillard House and the picture was taken in 1937. Much of the property in the street has now been demolished. Other buildings in the photograph include the Wheatsheaf Inn and the Queen's Arms. *(RI/374)*

Farmers casting an expert eye over the sheep at the Lincoln Fat Stock Associations Christmas Show, held at Lincoln Cattle Market in 1959. *(RI/3428A)*

Scothern, in 1939, with a scene many would travel miles today to see, with a steam-driven thresher and baler in use. *(RI/392)*

Former American Army trucks get a new lease of life under the ownership of C. A. E. C. Howard Ltd. Note the left-hand drive. *(RI/1260)*

A rural threshing scene at Grange-de-Lings in 1938. *(RI/390)*

Loading up the hay wagon at the end of a day's harvesting at Kettlethorpe in 1947. *(RI/402)*

A new giant silo under construction at Bardney sugar beet factory in 1956. *(RI/2046)*

Sugar beet being unloaded by hand at the Bardney factory in 1931. *(RI/538)*

A locally-built reaper being used at Digby in 1939, to gather a crop of lucerne. *(RI/529)*

Three horses pulling a reaper at harvest time in 1955 on Smith's potato estates, at Nocton. *(RI/865)*

Crop spraying was done by a horse-drawn sprayer in 1939, before aircraft and tractor-drawn machines came into general use. *(RI/531)*

An early form of combined harvester in operation in 1931. *(RI/465)*

This weird and wonderful looking machine is a gyrotiller at work in Martin Fen in 1934. *(RI/464)*

A mock trial being held at Ingham to mark the re-opening of the village stocks. *(RI/2639A)*

Ingham village stocks were reinstated in 1960 and the younger generation were able to see what life was like in the past for those who misbehaved. *(RI/2639)*

Four young hopefuls entering the Soap Box Derby held at Cherry Willingham in 1956. *(RI/1544)*

A casualty of the weather, this bus ended up in a ditch at the side of the road between North Hykeham and Aubourn. *(RI/1186A)*

The farm cat at Mr F. Reed's Greeve Farm, Broxholme, takes its daily drink of milk straight from the cow. *(RI/1270)*

Flood waters reached a depth of several feet after torrential rain fell in the Horncastle area in October 1960. *(RI/2662 B/A)*

Top, left: The old post mill at Hykeham Moor, built in 1756, had become a sorry sight in 1932 and it collapsed later in the decade and was cleared away. *(RI/361)*

Top, right: Metheringham's windmill started life with six sails, but as each sail was lost, the others were juggled around to keep the balance before it rather unusually ended its life with three sails. This picture was taken in 1938 after it had finished its working days. Because of its three sails, it became one of the most photographed mills in the county. *(RI/393)*

Left: Pocklington's Mill, Heckington, is the only eight-sailed mill in the country and is still in use today. It was built in 1830 and this picture was taken 102 years later. *(RI/360)*

A Lincoln-built Robey steam wagon putting in an appearance at the Carrington Traction Engine Rally in 1970.

A meeting of the Per Ardua Beagles, from RAF Cranwell, setting off from Navenby. *(RI/847)*

The Clock Tower and Embassy Centre are still there today in Skegness, but Butlin's House, on the left, has given way to shops, cafés and amusement centres. *(RI/1087)*

A local branch of the United Nations Association had their stall at a Lincolnshire Show in the 1950s. Prominent at the back is Mr Geoffrey de Freitas, who was MP for Lincoln from 1950 until 1962, when he was knighted and appointed High Commissioner in Ghana. Third from right is Mrs Mary Large, who for many years was a local councillor. *(RI/784B)*

The opening ceremony for the Hospital Fête, held at Metheringham, in 1936, was a colourful sight. *(RI/721)*

Taken in 1962, this view of Boston Market Place has changed little. The shops may have different names on them and the lamp standard on the roundabout, known as Five Lamps has been replaced with a modern, taller standard. St Botolph's Church is still the dominant feature. *(RI/4191A)*

Dunston Pillar was erected in 1751 by Sir Francis Dashwood (of the notorious Hellfire Club fame) as a land lighthouse, to guide travellers over the heath. The statue of King George III was put in place in 1810 and removed during the Second World War, when the height of the structure was lowered because of its danger to aircraft using the nearby Waddington Airfield. *(RI/293)*

Roundabouts for Boston's May Fair occupy the streets normally more used to cars, but the children don't seem to mind. *(78/894/15A)*

There was plenty of water in the Haven when this picture was taken at Boston in 1978. *(78/1074)*

Low tide in the Haven, at Boston, with some of the town's varied architecture visible beyond the far bank. *(76/744/B/20)*

Guests at the opening of Boston Arts Centre in 1978. *(78/894/8A)*

Mr H. H. Gurnhill, of Saxilby, with his 1928 Robey steam tractor, pictured in 1967. *(RI/2164)*

A host of admirers for this Marshall compound traction engine, built at Gainsborough and offered for sale at Saxilby in 1958. *(RI/2603)*

Sporting Memories

SPORTS and leisure play an important part of everyone's life at some time and these pictures will recall some of these activities.

Lincoln City FC have had ups and downs and some of these moments arc recalled.

Horse racing took place several times a year on The Carholme, Lincoln, until the mid-1960s and a whole host of sports and pastimes have been recorded in pictures.

It's a Knockout was a popular television show for many years, be it a sport or pastime. Lincoln featured in the programme on several occasions, once representing Great Britain in the international version *Jeux Sans Frontieres*.

Lincoln City FC's 1931-32 team who were Third Division North champions, gaining promotion to the Second Division.

Imps fans turned out in their thousands in 1952 when Lincoln City beat Stockport County and again won promotion to the Second Division. *(RI/819A)*

Celebrations in the boardroom when Lincoln City gained promotion to the Second Division in 1952. *(RI/819B)*

Lincoln City fans turned out in force to support the Imps, when they played at Barnsley in October 1955. *(RI/1449)*

Lincoln City's skipper in the 1950s, Tony Emery (left), with Graham Taylor, manager in the 1970s, when City gained promotion. Mr Taylor left Lincoln to manage Watford and then England. *(96/1832124)*

Nettleham FC met a team from Cardross, Dumbarton, Scotland, in August 1957. *(RI/3333)*

There was a covering of snow on the pitch when the White Horse football team was photographed on the West Common in February 1954. *(RI/1336)*

Top golfer Dai Rees giving a demonstration at Lincoln Golf Club, Torksey, in the 1960s. *(RI/1542)*

Lindum Cricket Club team who played Mr G. C. Wells-Cole's team during Lindum Cricket Week in 1958. *(RI/1518)*

Lincoln City FC manager Bill Anderson (second from right on front row) with his choice of local cricketers for a match against Woodhall Spa, in 1958. *(RI/1252)*

The Woodhall Spa team who took part in the match. *(RI/1764)*

Mr J. Wilkinson (left) and Mr A. Bosworth, who met in the Lincoln Amateur Billiards Senior Final in 1952. *(RI/1514)*

A line up of some of the competitors in the Lincoln Amateur Swimming Club's gala, at Boultham Baths, in 1963.
(RI/1516)

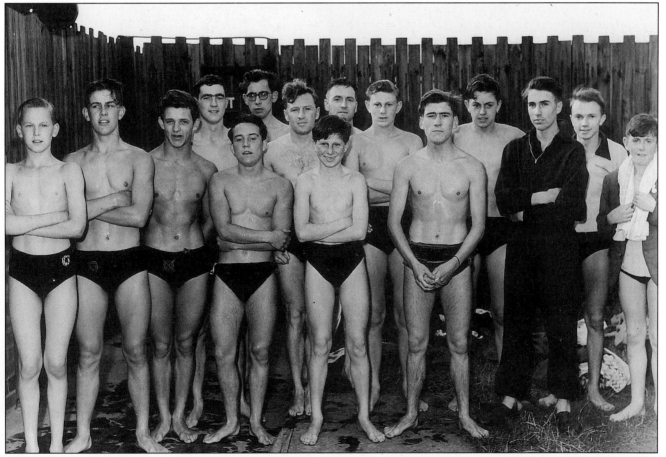

It didn't look particularly warm for these young swimmers at the Lincoln Amateur Swimming Club's annual gala in 1953.
(RI/1768)

The Hop Pole beat the Prince of Wales in the Warwick & Richardsons Darts League Final in 1955. On the right is the licensee of the Prince, Walt Rawlinson. *(RI/1757)*

The Roaring Meg played the Miller's Arms at darts in 1957, in the final of the Bascomb Cup competition. *(RI/1612)*

Wragby Road Social Club's Ladies 'A' Darts Team who won the Lincoln Clubs' Association Whitbread Cup in 1958. *(RI/1758)*

Table tennis was one of the activities at Reepham Youth Club in 1955. *(RI/2013)*

A whole lot of silver 'up for grabs' at the Lincoln Table Tennis Championship Finals at Kirke White Club in 1962. *(RI/1515)*

Competitors in a table tennis final held at St Botolph's Church Hall, in 1965. Second from left is John Radley, a prominent player in the area. *(RI/1775)*

Something seems to be amusing the onlookers during a fencing match between Lincoln and Grimsby in 1955. *(RI/1540)*

Spring Hill Girls' School netball team in 1954. *(RI/1538)*

Broadgate was the starting point for the Round Lincoln walking race in 1934. *(RI/491)*

A round of applause for the Cecil Thurlby, winner of the five-mile walking race, which ended at the West Common in 1935. *(RI/720)*

Lincoln Wellington Athletics Club team in 1956. On the back row are Jack Murphy (left) and Cecil Thurlby, well-known figures in the local athletics scene. *(RI/1536)*

Lincoln Wellington Athletics Club team, who competed in a field match against a team from the Royal Signals, in 1957. Identifiable on the picture are Ken Barnsdale (third from right, back row) and Ken Elkington (second from right, front row). *(RI/1608)*

Lincolnshire bowls team who played Leicestershire, at Branston, in 1955. *(RI/2007)*

Measuring up an end in the Carholme Cup bowls competition, played at the West Common in 1963. *(RI/1517)*

The three grandstands can be seen in this picture taken at The Carholme during the Spring Meeting of 1957. Today, only the grandstand on the left remains, converted into a Community Centre. *(RI/843A)*

The parade ring on The Carholme, for the Lincolnshire Handicap of 1933. What a wonderful collection of buses in the car park! *(RI/534)*

Gordon Richards rode Quartier Maitre in the Lincolnshire Handicap of 1940, on The Carholme. *(RI/588)*

A wonderful view of The Carholme, from the top of the grandstand, during Race Week in September 1949. *(RI/440)*

It was a very cold day in March 1964, when the Lincolnshire Handicap was run at The Carholme for the last time. Photographers lined up to picture the winner and on this group are *Echo* chief photographer Ken James (centre), *Echo* photographer Peter Washbourn (right) and, with the camera up to his eye, *Chronicle* photographer Derrick Kent, later to join the *Echo* staff. *(CVM)*

Lord Londesborough (left) and Lord Stanefield (right) at a meeting of the Blankney Hunt in 1935. *(RI/2045)*

Quite a crowd turned out for the opening of a roller skating rink in the former Astoria Cinema in 1957. *(2209)*

For a short while in 1960, Lincoln roller skaters had the best teachers in the country when Howarth Hargreaves and Sheila Wilkinson took over as 'professionals' at the Astoria. Sheila was Ladies Professional Figure Skating Champion and with husband Howarth, held the titles for Pairs and Dance skating. *(PW)*

Maurice and Pat Hodson, who taught many skaters roller dancing at the Astoria Skating Rink in the late 1950s and 1960s. *(PW)*

After the Astoria Roller Skating Rink had closed, the hall, formerly a cinema, became the Astoria Bingo Club, an 'eye's down' venue for many in the city. Now it is to become a branch of the Lincoln Co-operative Society. *(PW)*

Members of Lincoln Gliding Club ready for a day of flying at RAF Swinderby, in 1964. *(RI/2004)*

Lincoln motorcyclist Brian Freestone with his Norton motorcycle and some of the trophies which he won. *(RI/892)*

There were celebrations by the team and the cheerleaders when Lincoln beat Nottingham in *It's A Knockout*, in 1972, and later went on to take part in the international *Jeux Sans Frontieres* in Nice. *(Q726/B)*

Lincoln's team members in action against Nottingham. *(Q726/H)*

Cheerleaders making a lot of noise with rattles at the international *Jeux Sans Frontieres* in Nice, France, in July 1972. *(PW)*